Nuclear Security

The Hoover Institution gratefully acknowledges the following individuals and foundations for their significant support of this publication and the conference on which this book is based:

THOMAS AND BARBARA STEPHENSON

THE WILLIAM AND FLORA HEWLETT FOUNDATION

    PRESTON AND CAROLYN BUTCHER

    JOHN AND ANN DOERR

    THE KORET FOUNDATION

    THE MARY JO AND DICK KOVACEVICH FAMILY
       FOUNDATION

    WILLIAM AND SUSAN OBERNDORF

    PAUL AND SANDRA OTELLINI

    THE THOMAS AND STACEY SIEBEL FOUNDATION

NUCLEAR SECURITY
The Problems and the Road Ahead

George P. Shultz
Sidney D. Drell
Henry A. Kissinger
Sam Nunn

HOOVER INSTITUTION PRESS
STANFORD UNIVERSITY   STANFORD, CALIFORNIA

The Hoover Institution on War, Revolution and Peace, founded at Stanford University in 1919 by Herbert Hoover, who went on to become the thirty-first president of the United States, is an interdisciplinary research center for advanced study on domestic and international affairs. The views expressed in its publications are entirely those of the authors and do not necessarily reflect the views of the staff, officers, or Board of Overseers of the Hoover Institution.

www.hoover.org

Hoover Institution Press Publication No. 654

Hoover Institution at Leland Stanford Junior University,
Stanford, California 94305-6010

First printing 2014
20 19 18 17 16 15 14   7 6 5 4 3 2 1

Manufactured in the United States of America

The paper used in this publication meets the minimum Requirements of the American National Standard for Information Sciences—Permanence of Paper for Printed Library Materials, ANSI/NISO Z39.48-1992. ⊗

Cataloging-in-Publication Data is available from the Library of Congress.
ISBN: 978-0-8179-1805-7 (pbk. : alk. paper)
ISBN: 978-0-8179-1806-4 (epub)
ISBN: 978-0-8179-1807-1 (mobi)
ISBN: 978-0-8179-1808-8 (PDF)

Contents

Preface

George P. Shultz

Sid Drell, Sam Nunn, and I were invited to address the annual meeting of the American Nuclear Society in November 2013. This important organization of some 11,000 has worked constructively over the years on issues related to the use of nuclear-supplied energy. We were asked to speak about our long-standing interest in getting better control of the threats posed by nuclear weapons and reactors. Each of our papers addressed this issue in a different way. Sid Drell's paper is supplemented here by another paper he recently presented at Princeton's Institute for Advanced Studies. My paper is supplemented by two recent opinion pieces involving Iran, one coauthored by Henry Kissinger.

All three of us have been involved in nuclear security efforts for many years. Sid Drell, a physicist, has been a constructive force in arms control discussions, contributing his scientific expertise to understanding the true nature of the challenges involved and presenting ideas for how to deal effectively with them. My role began when I was President Reagan's secretary of state in the 1980s. During that period, we worked hard to reduce the number of nuclear weapons and we succeeded. Today, the number of nuclear weapons is on the order of 30 percent of their peak level in 1986. Sam Nunn, as chairman of the Senate Armed Services Committee, worked with Senator Richard Lugar to produce the Nunn-Lugar Cooperative Threat Reduction

Program that has made significant contributions to the security of the Soviet Union's, and now Russia's, nuclear stockpile and its orderly reduction. He now leads the Nuclear Threat Initiative (NTI) in its effective work on nuclear issues.

We all believe that further progress is urgently needed and that there are current initiatives that deserve strong support. An outstanding example is the series of meetings initiated by President Obama that brings together heads of state to focus on getting better control of fissile material. This effort is of critical importance because obtaining fissile material is the most difficult challenge to building a bomb. Progress is being made on other aspects of nuclear security, and consciousness of the problem is very much in the air. For example, under the leadership of Sam Nunn and the Nuclear Threat Initiative, a recent meeting in Singapore brought together established networks of knowledgeable people from Europe, Latin America, the United States, and the Asia-Pacific region who are working on nuclear security.

Our efforts to advance these issues will continue because, while the likelihood that a nuclear weapon will be used is low, the consequences of a single nuclear incident are enormous.

CHAPTER 1   Reducing the Nuclear Threat: Lessons from Experience

George P. Shultz

American Nuclear Society Meeting
November 11, 2013

My thesis:

1. The existence of nuclear weapons poses an existential danger to everyone in the world.
2. As we consider future developments, we must be ever vigilant of our, and our allies', national security interests. We emphasize steps, such as getting better control of fissile material, as marking the way forward. We know that as long as there are nuclear weapons, the United States must have an arsenal that is safe, secure, and reliable.
3. Great progress has been made since 1986 in sharply reducing the number of nuclear weapons and in creating an atmosphere where further progress seemed likely—a golden moment.
4. Right now, and rather abruptly, that atmosphere has changed sharply, with new threats of proliferation and use. So the question I put before you is: What can we learn from the earlier positive experience? What has gone wrong and where do we go from here?

Let me start with a brief history.

Concern about the threat posed by nuclear weapons has preoccupied the United States and presidents of the United States from the beginning of the nuclear era.

President Truman introduced the Baruch Plan—a radical call for international control of nuclear weapons. The plan was stillborn with Soviet opposition.

President Eisenhower, in a 1953 address to the United Nations General Assembly, called for negotiations to "begin to diminish the potential destructive power of the world's atomic stockpiles." He pledged that the United States would "devote its entire heart and mind to find the way by which the miraculous inventiveness of man shall not be dedicated to his death, but consecrated to his life."

At the end of the Eisenhower administration, the United States had 20,000 nuclear warheads and the Soviet Union 1,600. After the Cuban Missile Crisis, President Kennedy spoke eloquently in favor of a nuclear-free world. But at the time of his death, the United States had 30,000 nuclear warheads and the Soviet Union had 4,000.

President Johnson negotiated the Nuclear Nonproliferation Treaty and started what became the Strategic Arms Limitation Talks (SALT). But as he left office, China had tested a nuclear weapon to become the fifth nuclear state, and the Soviet arsenal had increased to 9,000 weapons.

President Nixon succeeded in negotiating the first limitations on strategic offensive forces, but by the time he and his successor, President Ford, left office, the US arsenal had 26,000 nuclear weapons and the Soviet Union's arsenal had grown to 17,000.

President Carter, concerned about nuclear weapons, negotiated a second SALT Treaty but withdrew it from the Senate in 1979 when the Soviet Union invaded Afghanistan. By the time he left office, the Soviet Union had 30,000 nuclear weapons and the United States, 24,000.

President Reagan, early in his administration, asked the Joint Chiefs to tell him what would be the result of an all-out Soviet attack on the

United States. The answer: it would wipe us out as a country. Would he retaliate? Yes. And he said many times, "What's so good about keeping the peace through an ability to wipe each other out?"

So Reagan decided on what was regarded as a radical and unachievable objective: he called for the elimination of intermediate-range nuclear forces (INF) (the Soviets had 1,500 deployed and the United States had not yet deployed any). He also called for cutting in half the number of strategic weapons on each side. He publicly advocated the goal of a world free of nuclear weapons. In 1983, the INF negotiations failed and the North Atlantic Treaty Organization (NATO) put into effect a prior decision to deploy intermediate-range weapons if negotiations failed. The Soviets withdrew from negotiations. Tensions rose. Talk of war filled the air. Reagan, early in 1984, spoke in a conciliatory way about prospects for a better world. Gradually, the situation settled down and arrangements were made for the resumption of the annual visit by Foreign Minister Gromyko to Washington at the time of the UN General Assembly, a practice that had been discontinued by President Carter after the Soviet invasion of Afghanistan.

Tensions began to subside and arrangements were made and successfully implemented in January 1985 to resume arms control talks. At this point, Mikhail Gorbachev came on the scene as the new general secretary of the Soviet Union. The first meeting between Reagan and Gorbachev took place in Geneva in November 1985. The main, and important, result was a change in atmosphere. The joint statement issued by Reagan and Gorbachev exclaimed, "A nuclear war can never be won and must never be fought."

At the time, Soviet warheads outnumbered US warheads, and the total number of nuclear weapons in the world, including Great Britain, France, and China, came to about 70,000. Then came Reykjavik.

Reagan and Gorbachev met in a small room in Hofdi House for two full days of talks. I was privileged to sit with President Reagan and my counterpart, Eduard Shevardnadze, was beside General Secretary Gorbachev. Momentous developments were discussed and potential agreements identified. We were on the way to agreeing on the elimination of intermediate-range weapons and cutting in half strategic nuclear arms to equal levels on a satisfactory bomber-counting rule. At the end, they did not close any deal at that time because Reagan and Gorbachev disagreed about the issue of strategic defense. Nevertheless, we had seen the Soviets' bottom line and the agreements subsequently came into effect. Little noticed at the time, but of deep significance, was an agreement reached in an all-night session between the first and second days of the meeting, negotiated by Roz Ridgway with Sasha Bessmertnyk, that human rights would be a recognized, regular item on our US-Soviet meeting agendas. This was a signal, not well recognized at the time, that the Soviet Union was ready for deeper changes, as subsequently advocated by Gorbachev.

I went to the United Nations on December 7, 1988, to hear Gorbachev give an address. The headline from his statement was the withdrawal of Soviet conventional forces from Europe, but I thought the most important message was that, as far as he was concerned, the Cold War was over.

The Cold War died, but died hard in the United States, as debate raged between President Reagan and me, observing that change was taking place in the Soviet Union, and others like former President Nixon and CIA Director Robert Gates, who thought we were wrong and naïve, and that the Soviet Union could not change. Our point of view prevailed in the end.

A golden decade or so followed, and by 2006, nuclear weapons had been reduced to about 30 percent of their numbers at the time of Reykjavik.

Following a conference at Stanford University's Hoover Institution, Henry Kissinger, Bill Perry, Sam Nunn, and I wrote an op-ed calling for a world without nuclear weapons and identifying steps needed to get there. The op-ed was received positively throughout the world. Prominent statesmen signed on. The UN Security Council unanimously adopted a resolution calling for the creation of the conditions that would lead to a world without nuclear weapons. Yes, there were objections, but the trend of opinion was clear. And in the campaign for the 2008 presidential election, both candidates, John McCain and Barack Obama, agreed on the goal of a world free of nuclear weapons, and both have continued their advocacy of this objective.

But something has gone wrong. The atmosphere has changed. Proliferation and the potential use of nuclear weapons have once again come to the fore as primary concerns.

So now I ask you two questions. What can we learn from observing the forces that led to the golden moment when huge reductions in nuclear arsenals took place? Can we identify the key ingredients for a road ahead that can lead us toward a world free of nuclear weapons?

Here are some lessons from the golden moment.

First of all, there was in place a long and deep sense of unease about the devastating capabilities of nuclear weapons. In an odd way, the Chernobyl accident reinforced this feeling. I was impressed that in my first meeting with Gorbachev after Chernobyl, I found he had asked the same question I had put to my colleagues in the United States: What is the relationship between the vast damage we see at Chernobyl and what would have been produced by a weapon? The answer: A weapon would be far more devastating. Fukushima is causing some similar anxiety, but it is easy for people to go to sleep on the issue. So the problem of danger, unfortunately all too real, needs to be kept in public view.

Second, there needs to be some leverage in the picture that helps the argument. In an odd way, President Reagan's Strategic Defense Initiative provided some leverage. Consider this statement: In a lengthy letter from Reagan to Gorbachev on July 25, 1986, after the Geneva meeting but before the Reykjavik meeting, he wrote:

> Significant commitments of this type with respect to strategic defense would make sense only if made in conjunction with the implementation of immediate actions on both sides to begin

moving toward our common goal of the total elimination of nuclear weapons. Toward this goal, I believe we also share the view that the process must begin with radical and stabilizing reductions in the offensive nuclear arsenals of both the United States and the Soviet Union.

Third, we need people at the top of key countries who can think big, act boldly, *and* carry their constituencies with them. This is difficult and takes a leader who will stand up to fierce opposition from a respected source. I remember vividly coming back to Washington from Reykjavik and practically being summoned to the British ambassador's residence where my friend Margaret Thatcher "handbagged" me. She said, "George, how could you sit there and allow the president to talk about a world free of nuclear weapons?" I said, "But Margaret, he's the president." "Yes, but you're supposed to be the one with his feet on the ground." "But Margaret, I agreed with him."

The idea was probably too bold for immediate implementation, but it was out there and some down payments emerged. The vote in the US Senate to ratify the INF Treaty eliminating intermediate-range nuclear weapons was 93 to 5.

Finally, and the real key, is the change in atmosphere. Beginning with Reykjavik and gradually rolling on, the Cold War came to an end, so whatever were the justifications for nuclear weapons diminished. People even began to look at the financial costs and think about how the money spent on nuclear weapons could be better used.

So what does this tell us about the road ahead?

First of all, we must have the ideas in place that can help us reach our goal, step by step. The ideas are there. They need to be publicized. For example, huge progress has been made in the ability to verify. Work is going on to get better control of fissile material. Agreements on verification are being reached, such as in the breathtaking arrangements for on-site inspection in the most recent US-Russia Strategic Arms Reduction Treaty (START). And progress is being made in other dimensions, such as the material on the Open Skies Treaty developed by Sid Drell and Chris Stubbs.

Second, there obviously needs to be hard work done on proliferation by Iran and North Korea and on sources of great tension such as those between Pakistan and India.

Third, we need to face the fact that the great post–World War II activation of a global security and economic commons is deteriorating badly, and we now find ourselves in a world awash in change. The uncertainty generated by this deterioration causes people to hang onto whatever they rightly or wrongly think will give them security.

The serious problem of governance right now is that diversity, long in existence but suppressed, is asserting itself as never before in a world of transparency—a world dominated by the information and communications revolution. We need to get back to the stability of a global economic and security commons, and that means learning how to govern over diversity in an age of transparency.

Finally, and of immense importance, is continued advocacy. At this point, religious leaders are coming together, based on the broad conviction that weapons of mass destruction are inhumane and incompatible with the basic principles of any religion. Other voices are being heard. The Nuclear Threat Initiative (NTI) has produced a compelling video documentary on nuclear weapons, and an effort is under way to organize influential groups in every part of the world. The Comprehensive Test Ban Treaty still needs ratification by the US Senate. We all need to keep ourselves informed and make ourselves heard in a sustained and often focused way.

The basic problem is that time is not on our side. We can hope and pray that we don't have to wait for the reality of the use of a modern nuclear weapon to realize how unacceptable these weapons are.

CHAPTER 2 **Challenges to Maintaining Trust in the Safety and Security of the Nuclear Enterprise**

Sidney D. Drell

American Nuclear Society Meeting
November 11, 2013

When I speak of the global nuclear enterprise, I include both nuclear weapons and nuclear reactors. It first moved out from the limited domain of nuclear scientists onto the world stage with the shock at the death and destruction caused by the two primitive atomic bombs that obliterated Hiroshima and Nagasaki. Each released more than a thousand times the explosive energy of the largest conventional bombs used in the devastating air raids during World War II, and they themselves have since been superseded by the thermonuclear, or hydrogen, bombs that release another factor of a hundred or so more destructive energy.

We have learned that these weapons can kill and destroy on an unprecedented, almost unimaginable scale. The existential threat of nuclear weapons to our civilization, as discussed by Secretary Shultz, has moved senior US leaders to call for efforts to free the world from living under their unparalleled danger of global destruction. And numerous religious leaders, statesmen, and scientists have echoed these words around the world.

We have also learned that the potential value of nuclear reactors to supply clean and safe energy is enormous. But they too can cause severe and unpredictable consequences to life in the event of an accident. But, it is unfortunate and dangerous that there is far too little public understanding of the realistic physical limits on the consequences of such accidents. This is evident in the global reaction to the Fukushima meltdown. Although the major part of the death and destruction was caused by the tsunami, created by an earthquake, Fukushima bears a grossly exaggerated blame in the eyes of the public. And the ongoing fumbling by the Japanese officials—both nuclear and governmental—unfortunately, but understandably, has further sullied the reputation of the nuclear enterprise. It is harmful for the future of the nuclear enterprise when an unprepared citizenry is so shocked by such events, and the leaders reveal inadequate preparation and commitment to deal with them.

In the twenty-seven years since the meltdown of the nuclear reactor at Chernobyl in the Soviet-era Ukraine, the nuclear power industry, both here and abroad, has strengthened its safety practices. And we can be proud of our positive record on safety. Over the past decade, growing concerns about global warming and energy independence have actually strengthened support for nuclear energy in the United States and globally. Yet despite these trends, the civilian nuclear enterprise remains fragile. Since Fukushima, opinion polls have given stark evidence of the public's deep fears of the invisible force of nuclear radiation. It is not simply a matter of getting better information to the public, but of actually educating the public about the true nature of nuclear radiation and its risks. Of course, the immediate task of the civil nuclear power component of the enterprise is to strive for the best practical safety and security record. The overriding objective could not be more clear: no more Fukushimas. Trust is fragile; once broken, trust is hard to regain!

We can also be proud of the positive record of safety and security of the nuclear weapons enterprise in the United States. We have built, deployed, exercised, and dismantled roughly 70,000 nuclear warheads, and there have been accidents involving nuclear weapons, but none that led to the release of nuclear energy. This was the result of a strong effort and continuing commitment to include safety as a primary criterion in new weapons designs, and also in careful production, handling, and deployment procedures. The key to the health of today's nuclear weapons enterprise is maintaining justifiable trust and confidence in the safety of its operations and in the protection of special nuclear materials—that is, fuel for bombs: plutonium-239 plus highly enriched uranium—against illegal sales or theft. One can imagine how different the situation would be today if one of the two four-megaton bombs that fell from a disabled B-52 Strategic Air Command bomber on airborne alert over Goldsboro, North Carolina, in 1961 had detonated (four megatons is approximately 260 times the explosive energy in the Hiroshima bomb). In that event, a single switch in the arming sequence of one of the bombs, by remaining in its "off" position while the aircraft and its electrical circuits were disintegrating, was all that prevented a full-yield nuclear explosion (see Figure 1). A close call, indeed. Fortunately, the strong and effective effort to improve the safety and security of our nuclear arsenal over the past fifty years—and continuing—has removed that and many other vulnerabilities to accidental detonations. It is disturbing, however, that incidents that occurred recently give evidence of a weakening security culture in elements of the nuclear military, such as the mistaken transfer of six nuclear-armed air-launched cruise missiles from Minot, North Dakota, that were carried airborne to Barksdale, Louisiana, with the absence of those nuclear warheads undetected for nine hours. In the past five years, several failures in security procedures were discovered at two Minuteman intercontinental ballistic missile (ICBM) bases, at Minot, in North Dakota, and Malmstrom, in Montana. Maintaining high security is complementary to, but equally important with, safety.

FIGURE 1. Four-megaton bomb dropped from disintegrating B-52 on airborne alert over Goldsboro, North Carolina, January 1961.

As a result of the global spread of nuclear knowledge, technology, and material, the nuclear enterprise of weapons and reactors is currently facing new and increasingly difficult challenges. These challenges were discussed in a conference we held at the Hoover Institution at Stanford University. Its findings and recommendations, as well as the papers prepared to help focus the discussion, are included in the book on the nuclear enterprise that Secretary Shultz and I published in 2012.[1] We examined risks and potentially deadly consequences associated with nuclear power and weapons and identified three guiding principles leading to four recommendations that are important for efforts to reduce those risks globally.

First, the calculations used to assess nuclear risks in both the military and the civil sectors are fallible. When dealing with very low-probability and high-consequence operations, we typically have little data as a basis for making quantitative analyses. Governments, industry, and concerned citizens must regularly reexamine the assumptions on which safety and security measures, emergency preparations, and nuclear energy production are based.

Second, there is a growing risk of accidents, mistakes, or miscalculations, and of regional wars or nuclear terrorism. States new to the nuclear enterprise may not have effective safeguards to secure nuclear weapons and materials or the capability to safely manage and regulate civil reactors. On the civil side of the nuclear ledger, the sobering paradox is this: While a reactor accident would be considerably less devastating than the detonation of a nuclear weapon, as is evident from Chernobyl, the risk of an accident occurring is probably higher. Currently, 1.4 billion people live without electricity, and by 2030 the global demand for energy is projected to rise by about 25 percent. With the added need to minimize carbon emissions, nuclear power reactors will become increasingly attractive alternative sources for electric power, especially for developing nations. These countries, in turn, will need to meet the challenge of developing appropriate governmental institutions and the industrial infrastructure, expertise, and

---

1. George P. Shultz and Sidney D. Drell eds., *The Nuclear Enterprise: High-Consequence Accidents—How to Enhance Safety and Minimize Risks in Nuclear Weapons and Reactors* (Stanford, CA: Hoover Institution Press, 2012). This talk draws on material in the introduction to that book, coauthored with George P. Shultz and Steven P. Andreasen.

experience to support a nuclear power enterprise with a suitably high standard of safety. This is true whether the decision is to continue to develop large high-power reactors or small modular models providing many distributed sources of power for the energy grid.

Third, no nation is immune from risks involving nuclear weapons and nuclear power within its borders. For example, since 1945 there have been more than thirty acknowledged serious accidents involving US nuclear weapons, mostly involving US Strategic Air Command bombers and earlier bomb designs not yet incorporating modern nuclear detonation safety designs. These are the so-called Broken Arrow events.

The United States has had an admirable safety record in its civil nuclear power program since the 1979 Three Mile Island accident in Pennsylvania, yet safety concerns persist. One of the critical assumptions in the design of the Fukushima reactor complex was that, if electrical power was lost at the plant and back-up generators failed, power could be restored within a few hours. The combined one-two punch of the earthquake and tsunami, however, made the necessary repairs impossible in such a short time. In the United States today, some nuclear power reactors are designed with a relatively short window for restoring power. After Fukushima, this is an issue that deserves action, especially in light of our own Hurricane Katrina experience in 2005, which rendered many affected areas inaccessible for days; and also the August 2011 East Coast earthquake that shook the North Anna nuclear power plant in Mineral, Virginia, beyond expectations based on previous geological activity.

In the light of these guiding principles, at the Stanford/Hoover conference we arrived at four related recommendations for reducing risks, which should be adopted by the nuclear enterprise, both military and civilian, in the United States and abroad.

First, the reduction of nuclear risks requires every level of the nuclear enterprise and related military and civilian organizations to embrace the importance of safety and security as an overarching operating rule. This means setting priorities in the proper order, based on bringing to bear the best analytic tools to analyze and understand risks and consequences, with the burden of proof resting on proving the system is safe, rather than being satisfied with lack of evidence that it is unsafe. This is not as easy as it sounds. To a war fighter, more safety and control can mean less reliability and availability, and greater costs. For a company or utility involved in the construction or operation of a nuclear power plant, more safety and security can mean greater regulation and higher costs. For both programs, enforcing accountability is essential.

Second, independent regulation of the nuclear enterprise is crucial to setting and enforcing the safety and security rule. In the United States today, the nuclear regulatory system—in particular, the Nuclear Regulatory Commission (NRC)—is credited with setting a uniquely high standard for independent regulation of the civil nuclear power sector. This is key to a successful and safe nuclear program. Effective regulation is even more crucial when there are strong incentives to keep an aging nuclear reactor fleet in operation, and to keep operating costs down. That combination could create conditions for a catastrophic nuclear power plant failure. Careful attention is required to protect the NRC from regulatory capture by vested interests in government and industry, the latter funding a high percentage of the NRC's budget. Strong, independent regulatory agencies are not the norm in many countries. Strengthening the International Atomic Energy Agency (IAEA) so that it can play a greater role in global civil nuclear safety and security would help reduce risks. This will require greater authority to address both safety and security, as well as adequate resources for an agency whose annual budget is only €333 million (US $421 million), with just one-tenth of that allocated for nuclear safety and security.

Third, independent peer review should be incorporated into all aspects of the nuclear enterprise. On the weapons side, independent experts in the United States—from both within and outside the various concerned organizations including the weapons labs—are relied on to review or "red team" each other, rigorously challenging and debating weapons and systems safety, and communicating these points up and down the line. Concerning reactor safety, the Institute of Nuclear Power Operations (INPO) provides strong peer review and oversight of the civil nuclear sector in the United States. Its global counterpart, the World Association of Nuclear Operators (WANO), should give a higher priority to further strengthening its safety operations, in particular its peer review process. What they can learn from the experience of the United States and other nations would help states entering the world of high-consequence operations to develop a culture and standard needed to achieve an exemplary safety record.

Fourth, progress on all aspects of nuclear threat reduction should be organized around a clear goal: a global effort to reduce reliance on nuclear weapons, prevent their spread into potentially dangerous hands, and ultimately end them as a threat to the world. As Secretary Shultz said, the very existence of nuclear weapons poses an existential danger to everyone in the world. Simply acquiring potential bomb fuels, plutonium-239 or highly enriched uranium—the so-called special nuclear material—is by far the most difficult step in building a relatively primitive, but deadly effective, nuclear weapon. And today the world is awash with nuclear materials. How long can we count on continuing to bat 100 percent in keeping these deadly weapons, or just their fuel, plutonium and highly enriched uranium, out of the hands of dangerous leaders and terrorists willing to resort to suicidal actions to achieve their goals? Establishing a world free of nuclear weapons that President Reagan advocated, a call that was repeated by President Obama in 2009 in his speech in Prague, is the only way to remove the risk they pose. Necessary steps toward achieving such a goal were discussed by Secretary Shultz in his opening talk, and will also be by Senator Nunn in the following one.

My bottom line: Since the risks posed by the nuclear enterprise are so high, no reasonable effort should be spared to ensure safety and security.

For all its utility and promise, the nuclear enterprise is unique in the enormity of destructive energy that can be released through blast, heat, and deadly radioactivity. Managing the nuclear enterprise is like holding two tigers by the tail, aware of the dangers and consequences if either or both shake loose.

This meeting of the American Nuclear Society is celebrating the seventy-fifth anniversary of the discovery of nuclear fission, and I have only talked about the dangers and catastrophic consequences of errors of commission and omission in handling elements of the nuclear enterprises. I much prefer to close on a positive note. To do so I will recall a little known but major error made in the discovery of nuclear fission. It may very well be responsible for the fact that we, not Hitler and the Nazis, won and survived World War II. An enormous benefit, indeed. Consider this chain of events:

The science of nuclear physics was born with the discovery of the neutron in 1932 by James Chadwick working in Lord Rutherford's lab in Cambridge, England. It was now understood for the first time what a nucleus was made of—neutrons and protons—a finding that cleared away many very troubling puzzles. One of the attractions of neutrons as a particle is that it carries no electric charge. Therefore there is no strong electric repulsion, no coulomb force, to prevent a beam of neutrons— emitted from radioactive nuclei and aimed at target nuclei—from penetrating into them. Previously physicists trying to explore into nuclei had to rely on protons or alpha particles emitted by naturally radioactive nuclei like radon and radium, which had been discovered by the Curies and colleagues around 1900. But these particles were positively charged electrically and therefore were repelled by the electrically charged protons in the target nuclei. Before the invention of high-energy accelerators, they did not have enough energy to overcome the electrical repulsion and smash their way into the target nuclei. The electrically neutral neutron could, however, and thus was able to probe forces that held neutrons and protons together in the nucleus. All we knew was that these nuclear forces were much stronger than electrical ones, which is why protons were drawn together to form heavy nuclei.

Enrico Fermi, the great Italian physicist, realized this and built in 1934 a major experimental program in Rome with a number of soon-to-be famous colleagues who bombarded systematically much of the periodic table of nuclei with neutrons. They proceeded from light to heavy, transmuting each element into neighboring ones as a result of neutron capture, or kicking out other N, P, or α particles. Fermi[2] and his team published their first report on "Radioactivity Induced by Neutron Bombardment" in March 1934. It was a real game changer. Eventually, as he worked his way up the periodic table to study the characteristics of induced radioactivity, Fermi came to uranium. Up until he reached uranium with ninety-two protons in its nucleus, elements generally transmuted into nearby elements. But when he got to uranium, the radioactivity induced was quite different. That caused much activity and big-time confusion.

In June 1934, Fermi published a second article about the "Possible Production of Elements of Atomic Number Higher Than 92." This was quite a puzzle, and although Fermi's marvelous and very productive experimental program earned him the Nobel Prize in 1938, he and his team had run into a dead end. Nuclei with very different properties from any of the known slightly lighter neighbors of U92 were emerging from the neutron bombardment. Fermi believed he had discovered transuranic elements for which he proposed names: 93, ausonium; 94, hesperium. In fact, he had discovered nuclear fission without realizing it.

His June paper led to a critical letter that appeared in September 1934 in a publication in German that was not in the mainline for physicists to read. It was called the *Journal of Applied Chemistry,* and its author

---

2. For more details on this sequence of events, see Richard Rhodes's magisterial *The Making of the Atomic Bomb* (New York: Simon and Schuster, 1987).

was a respected female German chemist named Ida Noddack. She and her husband were known for having discovered rhenium, a hard metallic element of atomic number 75. Her letter was entitled "On Element 93," uranium being element 92, and it seriously criticized Fermi's work, saying his "method of proof" for discovering post-uranic elements was "not valid" and that Fermi ought to have compared his new radioactive element with all known elements. Her letter said: "Any number of elements could be precipitated out of uranium nitrate with manganese and so instead of assuming the production of a new transuranic element," she added, "one could assume equally well that when neutrons are used to produce nuclear disintegrations some distinctly new nuclear reactions takes place which had not been observed previously." She recognized that in the past, elements were transmuted only to their near neighbor. But as she wrote, "When heavy nuclei are bombarded by neutrons, it is conceivable that the nucleus breaks up into several large fragments, which would of course be isotopes of known elements but would not be neighbors." That is, they would be lighter elements far down the periodic table. Since prior to that no one had ever found a nuclear disintegration creating elements far removed on the periodic table, her letter was not well received. Noddack had recognized that point. Unfortunately, that was part of the reason for the paper being neglected, because it was such a strange idea, and she never specifically suggested fission. At this time, Fermi's colleagues were insisting that it was "reasonable" to assume the atomic number of the resulting element should be close to the atomic number of the targets being bombarded. Fermi refused to believe Noddack, and the fact that she was not a highly respected and famous scientist, that the letter was published in a relatively obscure journal to physicists, and was written by a woman chemist, not a physicist, added up to three strikes. It meant that little attention was given to her paper. Furthermore, all theoretical calculations, based on what little was known at that time, suggested insufficient energy was available to break up nuclei.

The whole point of my telling this story is to wonder: what if the great Enrico Fermi, who received the Nobel Prize in 1938 for the enormous contribution made by his neutron experiments, had not made that mistake, and fission had been discovered in 1934, instead of four years later in 1938, by Lise Meitner, Otto Hahn, and Fritz Strassman? Would Hitler have had the bomb? Would atomic weapons have been available and used in the European campaigns during World War II? Who would have won? And would we be here now? This makes it clear how careful one has to be, and how unpredictable the consequences are when you are dealing with such enormous energies. We may have been very lucky!

CHAPTER 3

**Nuclear Risk:
The Race between Cooperation
and Catastrophe**

Sam Nunn
Former Senator
Cochairman, Nuclear Threat Initiative

American Nuclear Society Meeting
November 11, 2013

Thank you, Jim Rogers, for your introduction and for your outstanding leadership. I particularly want to thank Jim and all gathered here today for the work of this Society—helping the world benefit from the peaceful uses of nuclear science.

On this Veterans Day, I would also like to recognize one of our nation's most outstanding public servants and veterans, former Senator Pete Domenici.

I am delighted to join George Shultz, who addresses every challenge with energy, optimism, keen intellect, and wisdom. He is always looking to the future—with one exception. When George attended Henry Kissinger's ninetieth birthday party, he reflected, "Ah, Henry—to be 90 again!" I also thank Sid Drell for proving many times that a brilliant *theoretical* physicist can make a profound *empirical* difference in the security of his country and the world.

All Americans should be grateful for the remarkable work that the people in this room have done to improve and ensure safety and efficiency in the nuclear field. Preventing accidents is absolutely essential. The future of nuclear energy depends equally on security: preventing the theft of weapons-usable materials—either highly enriched uranium or separated plutonium—that could lead to a terrorist nuclear attack. Nuclear energy also depends on avoiding a dangerous future where a state acquires technology for peaceful purposes, then uses it for nuclear weapons. Safety, security, and nonproliferation are the three key links in the chain to ensure the benefits of the atom for humanity.

Two Steps for Greater Security

In January 2007, George Shultz, Henry Kissinger, Bill Perry, and I published an opinion piece in the *Wall Street Journal*. We called for reversing reliance on nuclear weapons globally as a vital contribution to preventing their proliferation into potentially dangerous hands, and ultimately ending them as a threat to the world. We are not the first to express the goal of ultimately eliminating nuclear weapons from the face of the earth. We follow several US presidents, including Reagan and Kennedy, on this path. Jim Rogers would call this "cathedral thinking."

In fact, for more than forty years, the Nuclear Nonproliferation Treaty (NPT), signed by 189 nations and supported by every US president since 1968, has enshrined the obligation of moving toward a world without nuclear weapons. However, the NPT, for all of its virtues and benefits to mankind, offers this goal without a path and without benchmarks. It declares the vision without the steps for getting there. That's why, in our *Wall Street Journal* piece, we went beyond the goal by outlining the practical steps required to *reach* the goal. We recognized that without the vision of a world without nuclear weapons, the steps will not be perceived as fair or urgent, particularly by nations without nuclear weapons. But just as important, without the steps, the vision will not be perceived as realistic or possible.

The NPT also leaves several other dangerous gaps. It declares what many interpret as an unrestricted, sovereign right to nuclear technology for peaceful purposes. But this happens to be the same technology that can lead to weapons that can destroy God's universe.

When the treaty was negotiated in 1968, the acquisition of fuel-cycle technology and know-how was presumed to be beyond the reach of all but a few countries, and it was believed that sensitive information related to the nuclear fuel cycle could be protected and contained. This presumption is long gone.

The NPT also fails to address nuclear security, because a terrorist group building a nuclear weapon was considered to be somewhere between unlikely and impossible.

Two of the ten steps we proposed in our original op-ed were particularly designed to begin to fill these large gaps. These steps are essential if the world is to prevent nuclear catastrophe and over time achieve the ultimate objectives of the NPT.

First, we must secure all nuclear weapons and materials globally to the highest possible standards.

Second, we must develop a new and improved approach to managing the risks associated with producing fuel for nuclear power.

First—nuclear materials security.

Today, the elements of a perfect storm are in place around the world: an ample supply of weapons-usable nuclear materials, an expansion of the technical know-how to build a crude nuclear bomb, and the determination of terrorists to do it.

This should be a grave concern for all of us. Terrorists don't need to go where there is the most material; they are likely to go where the material is most vulnerable. That means the future of the nuclear enterprise, including the future of the nuclear power industry, requires that every link of the nuclear chain be secure—because the catastrophic use of *atoms for terrorism* will jeopardize the future of *atoms for peace*.

Perspective is crucial. The enemy of nuclear security is not only complacency; it's also paralyzing pessimism. The message must go out that on nuclear material security, we are moving forward. Because of the cooperation between the United States, Russia, and other nations, the world has made progress in securing weapons-usable nuclear materials. Since 2012, seven states have completely eliminated these materials from their territories. Today, twenty-five countries possess these materials—that's half the number of states that had them in 1992. Also, more than a dozen states have recently taken important steps to better secure their nuclear materials and reduce their quantities.

The Department of Energy and Ernie Moniz deserve a lot of credit for this important work. We are fortunate to have an energy secretary like Ernie who understands both our energy sector and our security challenges—perhaps better than any other secretary we've had.

This security mission, however, is far from complete and, indeed, is a mission that, like safety, never really ends. There are still nearly 2,000 metric tons of weapons-usable nuclear materials spread across the world in hundreds of sites, some of them poorly secured and vulnerable to theft or sale on the black market. A small amount is sufficient to build a terrorist nuclear weapon.

We need to secure all of it to a high standard. Yet, stunningly, even though the destructive power of these materials in dangerous hands has the capacity to shatter world confidence and change society as we know it, there is no effective global system for how it should be secured. Let me repeat that. There is no effective global system for how weapons-usable nuclear materials should be secured.

In spite of the global threat posed by these materials, security practices of countries vary widely. Some states require strong nuclear security practices; others don't. Some states require strong measures to counter the risk of insider threat; others don't. Some facilities have armed guards on site; others have to call the police or military to respond and hope that they get there in time.

This is not a complete vacuum. Several important elements for guiding states with their nuclear security practices do currently exist, but they fall far short of what is needed. In particular, the international legal agreement for securing nuclear materials and its 2005 amendment don't define standards or best practices. Nor do guidelines for nuclear materials security issued by the International Atomic Energy Agency (IAEA). Standards imply obligations, but the IAEA guidelines are taken by most states as suggestions and not requirements. In addition, both the legal agreement and the IAEA guidelines cover only 15 percent of weapons-usable nuclear materials—those used in civilian programs. The remaining 85 percent of materials are categorized as military or noncivilian and are not subject even to these limited guidelines.

This lack of an effective global system for nuclear materials security stands in stark contrast to other high-risk global enterprises. For example, in aviation, countries set standards for airline safety and security through the International Civil Aviation Organization, which then audits state implementation of the standards and shares security concerns with member states. If your practices don't meet these standards, your plane isn't going to land in the United States, the European Union, China, Russia, Japan, India, Brazil, or most other places around the world.

Obviously, in an age of terrorism, the airline industry depends on this safety and security system for its economic viability, and countries depend on it to protect their citizens. Shouldn't the security of potentially the most dangerous material on the planet have an equally effective approach?

My bottom line—the world needs a nuclear materials security system in which:

1. All nuclear weapons-usable materials are covered.
2. All states adhere to internationally recognized standards and best practices.
3. States demonstrate to each other that they have effective security in place by taking reassuring actions, such as inviting peer reviews of their facilities using outside experts.
4. States reduce risks by decreasing their materials stocks and the number of facilities that house them.

These steps and many others will be demanded by an outraged world after we've had a nuclear security catastrophe. I suggest we take these steps now.

Let me turn to the second major challenge—the proliferation of technology to produce weapons-usable nuclear material.

The peaceful applications of nuclear science can play an indispensable role in our efforts to meet human needs in the twenty-first century. I favor civil nuclear power and believe that it must play a crucial role in our energy future and our environmental future. The promise of our nuclear future depends on how we manage our nuclear present.

As many as three dozen countries are reported to be interested in building their first nuclear power plant. Those that choose to make the nuclear fuel themselves rather than rely on the international market will be technically capable of producing materials for nuclear weapons. As you well know, the same basic technologies used to generate fissile materials for civilian purposes can be used for military purposes. This increases global risks, because the inherently dual-use nature of these facilities provides states with a latent nuclear weapons capability—which, of course, is what's going on right now in Iran.

While important steps have been taken to strengthen IAEA safeguards and to change the way states conduct nuclear trade, these steps are not enough.

The world has been reluctant to confront this question: Do we really believe that we can live securely in a system that poses so few constraints on any state's ability to produce weapons-usable nuclear materials?

Iran and North Korea are on the front burner. Both flagrantly violated the NPT by breaching their obligations to put their fuel-cycle facilities under safeguards. This question, however, is much broader because enrichment and reprocessing are not illegal per se under the treaty. Iran, in particular, has been the center of attention these last several days. An agreement with Iran that allows us to test and verify

Iran's claim that it has no intention of producing nuclear weapons is absolutely essential. Over the long term, however, we must work globally on new approaches to the fuel cycle, or we will continue to have future Irans and North Koreas, and the world will get increasingly dangerous.

The NPT resulted from an implicit bargain between its member states: Those states with nuclear weapons agreed to give up those weapons over time, in exchange for the states without nuclear weapons agreeing not to acquire them. In addition, the NPT protects the right of all parties to the treaty to develop, produce, and use nuclear technology for peaceful purposes. In fact, currently under the treaty, *any country* is free to acquire sensitive fuel cycle technologies and can produce unlimited amounts of these materials for civil purposes. In today's world, this is a big challenge.

The NPT has been, and will remain, the most important and essential framework for nonproliferation efforts, but unless we work to close its dangerous gaps, neither part of the NPT bargain will likely be fulfilled.

A few questions to consider:

- If we are serious about the need to close these gaps without damaging the civil nuclear enterprise, can we build consensus around new approaches to the nuclear fuel cycle?
- Can we put all commercial production facilities, in nuclear-armed states as well as nonnuclear weapon states, under international safeguards—not management, but safeguards?
- Can we operate facilities according to accepted and agreed principles and best practices?
- Can we ensure that any effort to cross the line from civil use into nuclear weapons development becomes apparent very early in the process?
- Can we develop approaches where access to and operation of these fuel-cycle facilities are no longer asserted as the sacred

right of individual states acting alone, including states that
already have such facilities?

The biggest obstacles are political, not technical. We have to find
a path away from the current paralyzing mentality of "have versus
have-not" states and recognize that all states have to make changes
for our individual and collective security. Those states that do not have
nuclear weapons will no doubt demand that the weapons states move
more rapidly to fulfill their end of the bargain—moving step-by-step
toward a world without nuclear weapons. They have a point, and this
means that both the vision and the steps are essential. Without both
moving in parallel, progress on either will be very slow, very difficult,
and very uncertain as global nuclear risks increase.

The Issue of Sovereignty

Closing these gaps will not be easy. The roadblock to more effective
nuclear materials security and to a more secure nuclear fuel cycle is
a concept of national sovereignty that is not consistent with today's
dangers. States opposed to global rules on nuclear security con-
tend that the responsibility for nuclear security within a state resides
entirely with that state. Countries resisting changes to managing
the nuclear fuel cycle cite their right to enrich and reprocess under the
Nonproliferation Treaty. Most countries with nuclear weapons will not
give them up step-by-step unless they're confident that their build-
down will not be met by others building up.

These arguments imply that we must increase nuclear risk to protect a broad definition of nuclear sovereignty. Is that really the case?
As I see it, this definition of sovereignty will not survive after the first
act of nuclear terrorism. Do we have to wait for such a disaster? The
stakes for both global commerce and global stability are high.

Let me give a vivid example. A couple of years ago, *Scientific American* magazine reported on a study that investigated the likely impact

of a hypothetical regional nuclear war between India and Pakistan using a hundred weapons. According to the computer models, more than twenty million people in the two countries could die from the blasts, fires, and radioactivity. Smoke from the fires would cover all the continents, diminish sunlight, and shorten growing seasons. Agricultural yields would decline around the world, and one billion people with marginal food supplies could die of starvation within ten years.

Even if you give this scenario a substantial discount—or even if you change it by assuming a limited terrorist nuclear attack rather than a regional nuclear war—one truth should be clear. The right to do whatever you wish with nuclear technology in your own country is no more compatible with global nuclear safety and security than "do-whatever-you-want" aviation rules would be compatible with safe and secure international air travel.

Fortunately, many countries support the idea of shared and effective responsibility. They understand that this call is not an abdication of sovereignty; it's an *assertion* of the prime obligation of a sovereign state—to protect its citizens from disaster. A concern for the fate of citizens in our own countries entitles—even obliges—leaders to insist on global standards for nuclear materials security and a more secure nuclear fuel cycle.

The Tasks and Call to Action

While much of the work in nuclear security is in the hands of governments, it is clear that they need more effective partners outside government. At the Nuclear Threat Initiative (NTI):

- We have helped promote the global agenda on securing nuclear materials.
- We launched an initiative—backed by $50 million from Warren Buffett now matched to a total of $150 million—to establish an international fuel bank so that countries can

have assured access to nuclear fuel as a back-up to the market—without spreading bomb-making technology around the globe. It is taking a long time, but hopefully will be achieved soon.

- We helped create the World Institute for Nuclear Security (WINS), an organization that provides a forum to share and promote best security practices among those responsible for nuclear material. WINS needs sustained support from government and industry to continue this critical work.
- We are engaged in a global dialogue that is bringing experts together from inside and outside of government and across the nuclear industry to determine how to design and build a global system for nuclear materials security.
- In 2012, we evaluated and benchmarked nuclear security conditions in 176 countries through a first-of-its-kind NTI Nuclear Materials Security Index. The next index will be released in January 2014.

We acknowledge, however, that NTI is a small, nonprofit organization with a limited budget dealing with global threats and global opportunities. The world needs members of the American Nuclear Society to be leaders in the field of security as you have been in safety. Your wisdom and experience are vital to the future of the nuclear enterprise and our security. Yes, government does have the primary responsibility, but you can help. We are in a new era; we must think anew.

In a recent *Washington Post* op-ed titled "Strategic Terrorism," former chief technology officer of Microsoft, Nathan Myhrvold, observed: "Throughout history, each new generation of weapons technology was deadlier and more lethal than its predecessor. More lethal weapons required larger investments and industrial bases. A single nuclear device could destroy an entire city, but it also cost as much as a city and was far more difficult to build."

Nathan makes it clear that the economics of weapons of mass destruction have radically changed and that today we face a different cost equation and a different world. With today's technology, a small number of people can obtain incredible destructive power with crude nuclear, biological, chemical, or cyber weapons. We must deal with this reality.

I close with this thought: We are in a race between cooperation and catastrophe. We must run faster. With your help and leadership, I am confident that we will.

CHAPTER 4

The Gipper's Guide to Negotiating

George P. Shultz

The Wall Street Journal
November 21, 2013

With US-led talks to curb Iran's nuclear program underway in Geneva this week, American diplomats would do well to take a few pointers from the Gipper—my former boss, Ronald Reagan, that is—on how to negotiate effectively:

1. Be realistic; no rose-colored glasses. Recognize opportunities when they are there, but stay close to reality.
2. Be strong and don't be afraid to up the ante.
3. Develop your agenda. Know what you want so you don't wind up negotiating from the other side's agenda.
4. On this basis, engage. And remember: The guy who is anxious for a deal will get his head handed to him.

Take, for example, the negotiations with the Soviets that began in 1980 in Geneva over intermediate-range nuclear forces (INF). Reagan's agenda after taking office in 1981: zero intermediate-range and shorter-range missiles on either side at a time when the Soviets had around fifteen hundred such weapons deployed and the United States had none. Impossible! How ridiculous can you get?

FIGURE 2. Still a smile despite tension on key issues. With Mikhail Gorbachev in Moscow. October 23, 1987.

When negotiations with the Soviets didn't move forward, the United States deployed INF in Europe, including nuclear-tipped ballistic missiles in West Germany. We, with our NATO allies, had upped the ante.

The Soviets walked out of negotiations. War talk filled the air. Reagan and America's allies stood firm.

About six months later, the Soviets blinked and negotiations restarted. We worked successfully on a broad agenda designed to bring real change in the Soviet outlook and behavior. On December 8, 1987, seven years after negotiations began, President Reagan and Mikhail Gorbachev signed the INF Treaty, whereby these weapons would be eliminated. So much for the impossible.

Apply these ideas to the Iranian problem—the regime's increasing nuclear capacity and its unacceptable behavior. The reality is that Iran is the world's most active sponsor of terror, directly and through proxies such as Hezbollah, and it has developed large-scale enrichment capacity that far exceeds anything needed for power-plant operations.

Worse, Iran openly expresses its intent to destroy Israel. The election of President Hasan Rouhani, a "moderate" in the eyes of some, may provide a slight opening. But don't bet on it. At this point, strength in the form of sanctions is taking its toll. As with the INF negotiations, the United States shouldn't be afraid to up the ante.

Tehran maintains that it wants nothing more than to produce nuclear power for its people, medical research, and the like. As former Senator Sam Nunn, currently CEO of the Nuclear Threat Initiative, said on November 11 in an address to the American Nuclear Society: "An agreement with Iran that allows us to test and verify Iran's claim that it has no intention of producing nuclear weapons is absolutely essential."

Moreover, if Iran has no intention of producing nuclear weapons, then Tehran should cease all uranium enrichment and immediately allow international inspections for verification. Nuclear materials for power and research facilities are readily available and have been offered to Iran for such purposes for years.

Do we have a fallback position? Yes. Allow Iran and the International Atomic Energy Agency (IAEA) to identify an existing Iranian enrichment facility that can supply what is needed for purely civilian use. Then make sure that all the other enrichment facilities and the heavy-water reactor in Iran are destroyed under international inspection. Once the job is done, sanctions will be lifted.

It has become a cliché, but it still holds true: Trust but verify. An impossible dream? Remember Reagan, who dreamed an impossible INF dream. What did the Gipper teach us? Dreams can come true when accompanied by a little reality, strength, and a willingness to engage.

CHAPTER 5

What a Final Iran Deal Must Do

Henry A. Kissinger and George P. Shultz

The Wall Street Journal
December 2, 2013

As former secretaries of state, we have confronted the existential issue of nuclear weapons and negotiated with adversaries in attempts to reduce nuclear perils. We sympathize with the current administration's quest to resolve the Iranian nuclear standoff through diplomacy. We write this article to outline the options as we see them emerging from the interim agreement for a policy based on the principle of "trust and verify."

For two decades, American presidents from both parties have affirmed that the United States is unalterably opposed to an Iranian military nuclear capability. They have usually added a warning to the effect that "all options are on the table" in pursuit of this policy. A clear trans-Atlantic consensus, a decade of International Atomic Energy Agency (IAEA) reports, and six United Nations Security Council resolutions have buttressed this position.

The interim nuclear deal with Iran has been described as the first step toward the elimination of Iran's ability to build a nuclear weapon. That hope resides, if at all, in the prospects of the next round of negotiations envisaged to produce a final outcome within six months. Standing by itself, the interim agreement leaves Iran, hopefully only temporarily, in the position of a nuclear threshold power—a country that can achieve a military nuclear capability within months of its choosing to do so. A final agreement leaving this threshold capacity unimpaired would institutionalize the Iranian nuclear threat, with profound consequences for global nonproliferation policy and the stability of the Middle East.

For thirty-five years and continuing today, Iran has been advocating an anti-Western concept of world order, waging proxy wars against the United States and its allies in Lebanon, Syria, Iraq, and beyond, and arming and training sectarian extremists throughout the Muslim world. During that time, Iran has defied unambiguous United Nations and IAEA demands and proceeded with a major nuclear effort, incompatible with any exclusively civilian purpose, and in violation of its obligations under the Nonproliferation Treaty in effect since 1970. If the ruling group in Iran is genuinely prepared to enter into cooperative relations with the United States and the rest of the world, the United States should welcome and encourage that shift. But progress should be judged by a change of program, not of tone.

The heart of the problem is Iran's construction of a massive nuclear infrastructure and stockpile of enriched uranium far out of proportion to any plausible civilian energy-production rationale. Iran amassed the majority of this capacity—including nineteen thousand centrifuges, more than seven tons of uranium enriched 3.5 to 5 percent, a smaller stock (about 196 kilograms) of uranium enriched to 20 percent, and a partly built heavy-water reactor that will be capable of producing plutonium—in direct violation of IAEA and Security Council resolutions.

Efforts to resolve this issue through negotiation have a long pedigree. They began in 2003, after the revelation that Iran had been secretly constructing a uranium-enrichment facility at Natanz and a heavy-water reactor at Arak. They have continued on and off in different permutations, with the Geneva negotiations the most recent and fullest expression.

The record of this decade-plus negotiating effort combines steadily advancing Iranian nuclear capabilities with gradually receding international demands. A negotiation begun by the EU-3 (Britain, France, and Germany, with the backing of the United States) started from the position that, in light of Iran's record of nondisclosure of nuclear matters and its noncompliance with UN resolutions, any Iranian uranium enrichment or plutonium-production capability was unacceptable. Following the revelation of the Natanz and Arak facilities, the IAEA board of governors adopted a 2003 resolution expressing "grave concern" and calling on Iran to "suspend all further uranium enrichment-related activities" and "any reprocessing activities." The resolution called it "essential and urgent" for Iran to provide unrestricted access to IAEA inspectors, and requested that Iran "promptly and unconditionally sign, ratify and fully implement" an additional protocol to its Nonproliferation Treaty safeguards.

Nearly every year since then, the Western powers—first through the EU-3 and then through the P5+1 (the permanent members of the Security Council, including China and Russia, plus Germany)— offered Iran diplomatic and technical inducements to take account of Iran's announced aspiration to become a technologically advanced country. These countries put forward programs of technical assistance and nuclear fuel for a verifiably civilian Iranian nuclear program.

Iran rejected the proposals and accelerated its nuclear efforts. It periodically engaged in talks but never dismantled any aspect of its enrichment infrastructure or growing stockpile of fissile material. Six UN Security Council resolutions passed in 2006, 2007, 2008, and 2010 condemned Iran's defiance and imposed sanctions, demanding an unconditional halt to nuclear enrichment.

The interim agreement reached on November 24, though described by all sides as temporary, thus represents a crucial test of whether the seemingly inexorable progress to an Iranian military nuclear capability can be reversed. In exchange for an estimated $8 billion in sanctions relief, Iran will freeze for six months its existing nuclear program and stockpile, but through an unusually circuitous mechanism that reflects its determination to continue to enrich.

Iran has been permitted during the interim agreement to continue to add to its existing stockpile of seven tons of uranium enriched to 3.5 to 5 percent with the proviso that this stockpile must be reduced again to its original level by the end of six months. (This means that Iran retains the additional enriched material throughout most of the agreement, adding to its leverage in the follow-up negotiations.) Iran has agreed to "neutralize" its small stockpile of 20 percent-enriched uranium by converting it to an oxide by the end of the agreement, though Iran retains the technical capability to enrich an equivalent stockpile at a later date. Progress on a heavy-water reactor and plutonium-reprocessing facility at Arak has been paused, though it appears that ancillary work on the site will continue. Daily inspections are stipulated to verify Iran's compliance while the interim deal is in force.

A modest benefit of the Geneva agreement is that it achieves, albeit temporarily, a small lengthening of the "breakout" time Iran would need to construct a nuclear weapon by several weeks, as described by administration spokesmen. American diplomacy in the next phase will need to grapple with the challenge that this gain has come at the price of a subtle but fundamental change in the conceptual basis of the nuclear standoff.

Until now, the UN resolutions and IAEA directives have demanded an immediate halt to all activities related to uranium enrichment and plutonium production, and unconditional compliance with an IAEA inspections regime as a matter of right. Under the interim agreement, Iranian conduct that was previously condemned as illegal and illegitimate has effectively been recognized as a baseline, including an acceptance of Iran's continued enrichment of uranium (to 5 percent) during the agreement period. And that baseline program is of strategic significance. For Iran's stockpile of low-enriched uranium is coupled with an infrastructure sufficient to enrich it within a few months to weapons-grade, as well as a plausible route to producing weapons-grade plutonium in the installation now being built at Arak.

Not surprisingly, the Iranian negotiator, upon his return to Tehran, described the agreement as giving Iran its long-claimed right to enrich and, in effect, eliminating the US threat of using force as a last resort.

In these circumstances, the major US negotiating leverage—the threatened reimposition and strengthening of sanctions—risks losing its edge. For individuals, companies, and countries (including some allied countries), the loss of business with Iran has been economically significant. Most will be less vigilant about enforcing or abiding by sanctions that are the subject of negotiations and that seem to be "on the way out." This risk will be enhanced if the impression takes hold that the United States has already decided to reorient its Middle East policy toward rapprochement with Iran. The temptation will be to move first, to avoid being the last party to restore or build trade, investment, and political ties.

Therefore, too, the proposition that a series of interim agreements balancing nuclear constraints against tranches of sanctions relief is almost certainly impractical. Another tranche would spell the end of the sanctions regime. It will need to be part of a final agreement.

The danger of the present dynamic is that it threatens the outcome of Iran as a threshold nuclear weapons state. If the six-month "freeze" period secured in Geneva is to be something other than a tactical pause on Iran's march toward a military nuclear capability, Iran's technical ability to construct a nuclear weapon must be meaningfully curtailed in the next stipulated negotiation through a strategically significant reduction in the number of centrifuges, restrictions on its installation of advanced centrifuges, and a foreclosure of its route toward a plutonium-production capability. Activity must be limited to a plausible civilian program subject to comprehensive monitoring as required by the Nonproliferation Treaty.

Any final deal must ensure the world's ability to detect a move toward a nuclear breakout, lengthen the world's time to react, and underscore its determination to do so. The preservation of the global nuclear non-proliferation regime and the avoidance of a Middle East nuclear-arms race hang in the balance.

American diplomacy now has three major tasks: define a level of Iranian nuclear capacity limited to plausible civilian uses and to achieve safeguards to ensure that this level is not exceeded; leave open the possibility of a genuinely constructive relationship with Iran; and design a Middle East policy adjusted to new circumstances.

Some adjustments are inherent in the inevitable process of historic evolution. But we must avoid an outcome in which Iran, freed from an onerous sanctions regime, emerges as a de facto nuclear power leading an Islamist camp, while traditional allies lose confidence in the credibility of US commitments and follow the Iranian model toward a nuclear-weapons capability, if only to balance it.

The next six months of diplomacy will be decisive in determining whether the Geneva agreement opens the door to a potential diplomatic breakthrough or to ratifying a major strategic setback. We should be open to the possibility of pursing an agenda of long-term cooperation. But not without Iran dismantling or mothballing a strategically significant portion of its nuclear infrastructure.

CHAPTER 6 **Is it Illogical to Work toward a World without Nuclear Weapons?**

Sidney D. Drell

Institute for Advanced Studies, Princeton
September 28, 2013

The question that is the title of this article is both important and timely and it triggers very controversial, and sometimes strongly critical, responses. For more than fifty years the United States' vast arsenal of nuclear weapons has been, and still is, widely viewed to be essential to our national security. To many of the mandarins of nuclear policy in this country, and around the world, an initiative to create a world without nuclear weapons is considered dangerous as well as a misguided fantasy.

Why? As best I can understand it, they fear disturbing what they see as a relative calm and smooth sailing with our current condition of nuclear deterrence based on mutual assured destruction, or MAD as it is appropriately called. But in order to arrive at this conclusion, it is necessary to minimize, if not totally ignore, a growing danger. With the broad spread of nuclear technology and material, we are now facing an increasingly serious hazard that these weapons may be acquired, and used, by dangerous leaders and terrorists willing to resort to suicidal actions to achieve their goals.

Is it really logical to accept such risks, and to put our survival in the hands of rogue leaders or terrorists, should they acquire nuclear weapons by whatever means—theft, bribery—or more simply just acquiring the nuclear fuel itself, that is plutonium-239 and highly enriched uranium? Acquiring that material is by far the most difficult step in building a relatively primitive, but deadly effective, nuclear weapon. And the world today is awash with nuclear material. How long can we count on continuing to bat 100 percent in keeping that fuel, or these deadly weapons, out of the hands of such people, and preventing their use?

Against such dangers, nuclear weapons are no longer much of a deterrent. I am unable to think of any scenario in which the use of nuclear weapons would be appropriate or effective in dissuading their being used on suicidal missions, or in regional crises. On the other hand, I have no trouble thinking of one or two primitive bombs, like those that obliterated Hiroshima and Nagasaki, being detonated in New York, London, Paris, Moscow, or Beijing. And what do you think would be its global impact on the morning after, especially in large urban areas?

Through the decades of the Cold War, the United States and the Soviet Union—confronting one another as hostile adversaries—built enormous nuclear arsenals containing tens of thousands of nuclear weapons; most, by the way, are so-called H-bombs, orders of magnitude more powerful than the primitive bombs that destroyed Hiroshima and Nagasaki. The two adversaries relied on nuclear deterrence to avoid a war that would have resulted in their total mutual assured destruction. The common interest of the United States and the Soviet Union to survive offered some comfort as we tottered perilously along the brink of catastrophe; and we did succeed in deterring a nuclear holocaust during the Cold War. But today the Soviet Union no longer exists as an actively hostile adversary. It disappeared into the dustbin of history twenty-two years ago. What else did nuclear weapons deter? Not the Korean War, not the squashing of the Hungarian and Czech uprisings. We have recently marked the fifty-first anniversary of the Cuban Missile Crisis, but there were other frighteningly close calls during the Cold War, including false alarms and serious accidents, several that actually came perilously close.

Prior to the era of nuclear weapons, deterrence made good sense as a strategy for negotiating and compromising, as appropriate, to avoid direct armed conflict by all diplomatic means. But once the thermonuclear weapons turned deterrence into nuclear deterrence or MAD, such weapons brought great unprecedented dangers. These dangers were recognized early on. As stated bluntly by President Eisenhower in 1956, war in the nuclear age will no longer end with "exhaustion of the enemy and surrender, but with destruction of the enemy and suicide." George Kennan expressed eloquently what is required to escape this fate in his 1981 book, *The Nuclear Delusion: Soviet-American Relations in the Atomic Age*: "I can see no way out of this dilemma other than by a bold and sweeping departure, a departure that would cut surgically through the exaggerated anxieties, the self-engendered nightmares, and the sophisticated mathematics of destruction in which we have all been entangled over these recent years, and would permit us to move, with courage and decision, to the heart of the problem."

President Ronald Reagan and Soviet General Secretary Mikhail Gorbachev picked up on this theme when they first met four years later in Geneva in 1985, and agreed to the statement frequently repeated since then, that "a nuclear war cannot be won, and must never be fought." This led to a critical turning point in the US-Soviet nuclear competition one year later in 1986 at their remarkable summit in Reykjavik, Iceland. Reagan and Gorbachev spent two days in intense and painfully frustrating discussions in an effort to reach a formal agreement committing the United States and the Soviet Union to embrace the goal of a world with no nuclear weapons at all. In the end, they couldn't close the deal in what George Shultz, who was at Reykjavik with Reagan, called "the highest stakes poker game ever played." The cooperation and trust between the two countries that would be required to work together toward achieving this goal simply didn't exist; and the hope for that agreement faltered on their failure to reach agreement on how to limit work on ballistic missile defense systems. I will return to that issue shortly.

The very notion of removing all nuclear weapons discussed at Reykjavik caused a huge furor among many of the nuclear mandarins who considered it dangerous and heretical. British Prime Minister Margaret Thatcher flew to Washington immediately after the summit to see President Reagan. When she arrived she summoned the secretary of state, George Shultz, to the British Embassy and went at him, saying, "George, how can you sit there and allow the president to agree to abolish nuclear weapons?" He responded, "But Margaret, he's the president," to which she replied, "Yes, but you're supposed to be the one with his feet on the ground," to which George replied, "Margaret, I agree with him."

Despite their failure to close a deal, the Reykjavik Summit was an important event. The two leaders who had the power to launch 98 percent of the existing nuclear weapons had committed themselves publicly and officially to start reducing nuclear arsenals—and indeed one year later negotiated the removal of all of the several thousand intermediate-range (500–5,500 km) nuclear missiles based in Europe and around the world. Reykjavik also led to important progress in reducing the total number of nuclear bombs that today number less than one-third of their peak in 1986 of close to 70,000. But the numbers of remaining nuclear weapons are still staggering—in the many thousands for both the United States and Russia, which still possess more than 90 percent of all the existing nuclear bombs. We remain caught in the Cold War trap of nuclear deterrence more than two decades after the demise of the Soviet Union.

A growing concern that the world seemed to be inexorably approaching a tipping point with nuclear proliferation getting out of control moved George Shultz and me at Stanford to action eight years ago. We enlisted three distinguished former senior US government leaders with impeccable records, like George, as Cold War hawks—Sam Nunn, Henry Kissinger, Bill Perry—to join us, and organized a conference on the twentieth anniversary of Reykjavik, October 10–11, 2006. Our three goals were: 1) see what we could learn from that experience; 2) figure out what conditions would be required to convince ourselves and others that a more stable and peaceful world can be established without nuclear weapons, instead of trying to preserve a two-tier system, as it is today, with some nations with nuclear arms and others without, a world that a growing number of nations are rejecting; and 3) build a global constituency, a coalition of the willing, to work together to pave a practical path toward achieving such a goal as both desirable and realistic.

Out of that and subsequent conferences at Stanford and overseas, including colleagues from Europe and Asia, there emerged specific proposals of what we concluded had to be done to move these ideas ahead. What we learned from these discussions and conferences led to talks and publications, the most effective of which were op-eds in the *Wall Street Journal.* The first one, which appeared in January 2007, proposed concrete steps toward achieving the goal of a world without nuclear weapons. It generated a strong worldwide response that was enthusiastically positive, and gained public endorsement by two-thirds of the living former US secretaries of state and defense and national security advisers. Most importantly our work revived interest in pursuing the long-dormant Reykjavik goal of elimination of all nuclear weapons. An encouraging atmosphere was created.

Two years later, in 2009, President Obama added enormous weight to this call in his speech in Prague. He declared that "the existence of thousands of nuclear weapons is the most dangerous legacy of the Cold War," pledged to "put an end to Cold War thinking," and emphasized "America's commitment to seek the peace and security of a world without nuclear weapons." Obama also recognized that this would be an enormous challenge, politically and technically, because it won't be a return to the world as it was prior to Hiroshima and Nagasaki. The genie is out of the bottle; nuclear weapons can be built, have been built, and they cause devastating damage.

In order to make progress in achieving this vision, we must face the challenge of answering this key question: Is it possible to make the case that a world free of nuclear weapons is consistent with establishing a strategic stability among nations on a global scale? By strategic stability, I mean conditions discouraging breakout—that is, discouraging the reconstitution of even a very small nuclear arsenal—while also providing assurances that we could respond effectively to any such attempt at breakout rapidly enough to be confident of being able to defeat it.

Getting to zero and monitoring the end state will require achieving an unprecedented degree of international cooperation and transparency, and improvements in verification tools. Having just a handful of nuclear weapons illegally could make a big difference. Beyond reconnaissance from our earth-circling satellites, it will require close monitoring of all activities related to maintaining a nuclear weapons enterprise. This includes data exchanges, on-site inspections (both challenge and scheduled ones), tags and seals, and sensors to detect effluents. Yes, this is a daunting challenge; however, before dismissing the challenge as unachievable, consider it in the context of what we have already accomplished in developing cooperative means of verification with the Russian Federation.

Before the collapse of the Soviet Union twenty-two years ago, proposals for agreements to penetrate their iron curtain of secrecy and count the number of nuclear warheads on their deployed intercontinental ballistic missiles would have been laughed out of school. But that, and other related reciprocal inspections, is precisely what we negotiated, and that we are doing today in the New Strategic Arms Reduction Treaty (START) that entered into force in February 2011. This was a major step forward, the culmination of progress in this direction following the Reykjavik summit. We have come very far in the last two decades, and there is no reason to view this as the end of the line. The operational progress in this cooperation is proceeding on course.

This success of New START negotiation with the Russian Federation provides a template for efforts to identify and implement multinational initiatives that are perceived as necessary to establish and maintain strategic stability in a world without nuclear weapons. In order to generate a serious commitment from the nations around the world to work toward that goal, it must be understood as being credible, as well as desirable. In addition, the United States must maintain, with each step along the way, the confidence of our allies who rely on our military strength and political will as their nuclear umbrella.

On the positive side, it also is important to recognize that during the time it will take to surmount obstacles, and to negotiate and implement steps toward the end state of a world without nuclear weapons, we can anticipate a steady accumulation of vital information that will be gained not only through normal means of monitoring, but also as a result of the necessarily close working relationship among inspectors and technical personnel of the nations involved. That will be valuable.

An important initiative of this type, announced by President Obama, is an expanded international effort to put all special nuclear material—that is, potential bomb fuel—around the world under safe control within the next four years. He gave this a formal start in 2010 when he hosted forty-seven national leaders in Washington who committed themselves to this goal, with a follow-on meeting, two years later in 2012, in Seoul, Korea, of more than fifty leaders, which recorded significant progress. A third conference is now being prepared for next year in the Netherlands to check on how well we have achieved our goal. Progress in this effort is a big deal. It should receive adequate support to persist.

Similar efforts are underway to gain universal support for efforts to toughen the verification teeth of the Nonproliferation Treaty (NPT) that entered into force in 1970, was extended indefinitely in 1995, and, as of this summer, has been ratified by 189 nations—all but India, Israel, North Korea, and Pakistan, latecomers to the nuclear club. The NPT "obligates all parties to pursue negotiations in good faith to nuclear disarmament." It insures the rights of all parties to produce and use nuclear energy for peaceful purposes without discrimination. It also forbids transfer of nuclear weapons technology between nuclear and non-nuclear weapons states. The new effort to toughen the verification teeth of the Nonproliferation Treaty with an additional protocol has thus far been endorsed by 141 of the treaty signatories, and work is proceeding to make it an all-inclusive mandatory commitment. Beyond the Nonproliferation Treaty, efforts are in progress to establish international control of the nuclear fuel cycle—including, in particular, control of the nuclear fuel itself—and to negotiate a verifiable cutoff on the production of fissionable material for bombs. There's work to be done.

I will mention briefly two major issues where actions by the United States are needed to advance our strategic vision. They would surely contribute to restoring the encouraging atmosphere generated by President Obama in his Prague speech in 2009. The first one is the Comprehensive Test Ban Treaty (CTBT). President Clinton was the first signatory when it was negotiated in 1996. Currently it is signed by 183 nations and ratified by 161. There are forty-four so-called Annex 2 nations that have demonstrated a nuclear capacity and that must ratify the CTBT before it enters into force. Thirty-six have done so. The eight delinquents are India, Pakistan, North Korea, Israel, China, Egypt, Iran, and the United States. We are not in good company. All of our NATO Allies, plus the Russian Federation and Japan, have ratified it. It is believed that China will join us once we do. Every technical reason, not to mention the political/strategic ones, supports US ratification: This is the conclusion of the most recent detailed technical study by the US National Academy of Sciences issued last year. As a result of the deeper understanding of the scientific processes during a nuclear explosion that we have gained from a strong science-based

Nuclear Stockpile Stewardship Program at the weapons labs since 1992, when the United States performed its last explosive underground test, I personally believe not only can we be confident in the arsenal's safety and reliability, but my confidence is even higher than it was seventeen years ago, when the United States signed it. And that is not just a casually offered judgment.

Moreover, the academy report concludes that the CTBT International Monitoring System will be able to detect explosive tests robust enough to lead to developments inimical to US security interests. It will be enhanced by data from national systems once the treaty enters into force. I believe it is fully consistent with US interests to ratify this treaty when it comes up again for the Senate's advice and consent. It will constitute an important step in advancing, with US leadership, the global strategic commitment to achieving a world without nuclear weapons.

A second important issue for the United States and Russia to resolve is the strain between them over plans to develop and deploy ballistic missile defense (BMD) systems. I believe this is no more than political sparring. Forty years ago it was realized, albeit reluctantly, that any technically feasible BMD system can be overpowered simply by increasing the firepower of the attacking offensive missile force and doing so more readily and cheaply. That is still true today and is recognized by top government officials and scientists, including by the Russian deputy prime minister, Dimitry Rogozin, who recently stated that Russia will have no trouble penetrating US planned defenses; nor does the United States think differently.

When President Reagan in 1983 called on "the US scientific community who gave us nuclear weapons to apply their great talents to render them impotent and obsolete," his words, standing alone, invited an interpretation as a call for a major effort to create a bold new BMD system—an impenetrable multilayer astrodome against thousands of Soviet missiles and warheads. That is precisely how they were aggressively interpreted by many in his administration, especially the Pentagon and some of their scientific advisers, who immediately set out to design and build a so-called Star Wars shield. Their grossly excessive claims and promises were subsequently defeated by unaccommodating laws of nature.

We now know from an extensive literature of Reagan's public statements and private documents, many first released to the public in recent years, that Reagan was in fact a deeply committed nuclear abolitionist. That was, without a doubt, his vision, in a remarkable seven-page letter he wrote directly to Gorbachev on July 25, 1986, some eleven weeks before the Reykjavik Summit. Here is an excerpt:

> I believe you would agree that significant commitments of this type with respect to strategic defenses would make sense only if made in conjunction with the implementation of immediate actions on both sides to begin moving toward our common goal of the total elimination of nuclear weapons. Toward this goal, I believe we also share the view that the process must begin with radical and stabilizing reductions in the offensive nuclear arsenals of both the United States and the Soviet Union.

The role for ballistic missile defense that Reagan clearly had in mind and expressed in that 1986 letter, if not evident in his 1983 "Star Wars" speech or in his administration's subsequent actions, was limited to providing protection against a small number of missiles, and thereby countering a very limited threat, retained or rebuilt covertly, by a treaty violator. Such a limited defensive capability is key to achieving strategic stability by being able to counter efforts to reconstitute covertly. It is both a practical and important goal. If only the two countries had developed a level of mutual trust in 1986 to accept these words as meaning precisely what they said! Today, their importance cannot be denied or deferred.

In view of the decreasing value and increasing hazards of the current condition of nuclear deterrence, achieving the vision of a world without nuclear weapons is an urgent challenge. The answer to the question in the title of this talk is a resounding NO! Furthermore it is a fundamental moral challenge when you consider the consequences of failure: an unparalleled massacre of millions of innocent people, if not the very end of our civilization.

The dilemma we face today in our posture of mutual assured destruction, MAD, is superbly summed up by Father Bryan Hehir, a leading scholar on this subject, in a speech at Stanford University in 1987:

> For millennia people believed, but if anyone had the right to call the ultimate moment of truth, one must name that person God. Since the dawn of the nuclear age we have progressively acquired the capacity to call the ultimate moment of truth and we are not gods. But we must live with what we have created.

Final Thoughts

Recent tensions, punctuated by Russia's acquisition of Crimea and attendant events, increase the sense of uncertainty that has pervaded much of the world in recent years.

Uncertainty can easily hinder important steps to improve security. Right now, for example, a major effort is under way to get much better control of fissile material. The third summit on this subject was held in the Netherlands in late March. All three summits were attended by heads of government, underlining the seriousness of this issue. The very fact that the meeting took place is a positive sign. Time will tell about the ability of countries too often pulling apart to pull together and follow through on commitments.

We note, with our own reservations, commentary along the lines that the Ukraine must now regret having given up its major stockpile of nuclear weapons. With both India and Pakistan adding to their supplies, China opaque, and North Korea brandishing its weapons, we see the world heading in the wrong direction, a fact that will be highlighted if Iran produces a nuclear weapon, followed by the likely acquisition of nuclear weapons by Saudi Arabia and, perhaps, other countries.

All of these unwelcome developments emphasize the importance of maintaining the effort to gain better control over the nuclear threat and eventually to end it by eliminating the weapons themselves. President Reagan and General Secretary Gorbachev agreed in 1985 that "a nuclear war can never be won and must never be fought." As Reagan said in his 1986 letter to Gorbachev, "The overall aim should be the elimination of all nuclear weapons."

Time is not on our side, so let us be sure that we use that time wisely and effectively.

About the Authors

Sidney D. Drell is a senior fellow at the Hoover Institution and professor emeritus of theoretical physics at the SLAC National Accelerator Laboratory, Stanford University. For many years he has advised the government on technical national security issues as a member of JASON, and on advisory committees, including the President's Foreign Intelligence Advisory Board and Science Advisory Committee. His honors include the National Medal of Science presented by the president, a MacArthur Foundation Prize Fellowship, the National Intelligence Distinguished Service Medal, and election to the National Academy of Sciences.

Henry A. Kissinger served as US Secretary of State (1973–1977) and National Security Advisor (1969–1975). At present, Dr. Kissinger is chairman of Kissinger Associates, Inc., an international consulting firm. He has served as a member of the Defense Policy Board, Department of Defense, since 2001. Dr. Kissinger was study director in Nuclear Weapons and Foreign Policy at the Council of Foreign Relations and director of the Harvard Defense Studies Program (1958–1971). He received a Bronze Star from the US Army in 1945 and was awarded the Nobel Peace Prize in 1973, the US Medal of Freedom in 1977, and the Medal of Liberty in 1986. Dr. Kissinger is the author of several books and has also published numerous articles on US foreign policy, international affairs, and diplomatic history. His column, syndicated by Tribune Media Services International, appears in leading US and international newspapers.

Sam Nunn is cochairman and chief executive officer of the Nuclear Threat Initiative (NTI), a nonprofit, nonpartisan organization working to reduce the risk of use and prevent the spread of nuclear, biological, and chemical weapons. He served as a US senator from Georgia for twenty-four years (1972–1996). In addition to his work with NTI, Senator Nunn has continued his service in the public policy arena as a distinguished professor in the Sam Nunn School of International Affairs at Georgia Tech and as chairman of the board of the Center for Strategic and International Studies in Washington, DC. He is a board member of The Coca-Cola Company and is retired from the law firm of King & Spalding.

George P. Shultz, the Thomas W. and Susan B. Ford Distinguished Fellow at the Hoover Institution, has had a distinguished career in government, academia, and business. He is a professor emeritus in Stanford University's Graduate School of Business and has held four cabinet posts, most notably as secretary of state (1982–1989). He also served as secretary of labor and the Treasury, was director of the Office of Management and Budget, and was president and director of the Bechtel Group Inc.

Index